Contents

W9-AVL-278

Dear Child,

This is a very special time for you. You are preparing to take another step in your journey of friendship with Jesus and the Church. Your journey began when you were baptized. This journey of faith never ends. You will keep growing in your friendship with Jesus and the Church for your whole life.

Sometimes on our journey with Jesus we act in ways that hurt our friendship with him. We are sorry and want to be forgiven. We want to change and grow even closer to him. The Church gives us the Sacrament of Reconciliation to help us know that God forgives us and brings us back to him.

You are getting ready to celebrate the Sacrament of Reconciliation for the first time. In this sacrament, Jesus forgives your sins through the actions and prayers of the priest.

In *Call to Celebrate: Reconciliation*, you will

• learn that God is a God of mercy and forgiveness

• pray with your classmates and family

• listen to the stories of Jesus and the Apostles

• learn how to celebrate the Sacrament of Reconciliation

What is one thing you would like to learn this year?

_____

_____

_____

Chapter 1

We Are Called

We Gather

Procession

As you sing, walk forward slowly. Follow the person carrying the Bible.

🎼 Sing together.

> We are called to act with justice,
>   we are called to love tenderly.
> We are called to serve one
>   another,
>   to walk humbly with God!

We Are Called, © David Haas, GIA Publications

Leader: Let us pray.

Make the Sign of the Cross together.

We Listen

Leader: A reading from the Acts of the Apostles.

Read Acts 17:16–34.

The word of the Lord.

All: Thanks be to God.

Sit silently.

Leader: Let us call to mind the goodness of God, who gives us all good things. God gives us life and breath, and in him we live and move and have our being.

Come to the water to be marked with the Sign of the Cross.

Leader: [Name], God calls you by name to live in love with him always.

Child: Amen.

Leader: Let us join in the prayer that Jesus has taught us.

Pray the Lord's Prayer together.

We Go Forth

Leader: Loving God, our source of life, bless us, protect us from all evil, and bring us to everlasting life.

All: Amen.

Sing the opening song together.

3

God Calls

SIGNS OF FAITH

Baptismal Name

We are each given a special name at **Baptism**. Usually it is the name or some form of the name of a saint or Mary, the Mother of Jesus. It may be the name of an Old Testament person. The name given at Baptism does not have to be a saint's name.

Reflect

Signing with the Cross   Think and write about the celebration.

When I heard my name

_____

_____

_____

The part of the prayer that made me happy was

_____

_____

_____

This is what the prayer told me about God:

_____

_____

_____

God's Children

At our Baptism the priest or deacon calls us by name. The whole community welcomes us with great joy. We are baptized in the name of the Father, the Son, and the Holy Spirit. The priest or deacon makes the Sign of the Cross on our forehead. The Sign of the Cross is a sign we belong to God.

God calls us to a life of happiness with him. He promises us his grace. **Grace** is a sharing in God's own life. Imagine that! God wants us to be his children. He chooses us and wants us to love him and each other.

SIGNS OF FAITH

Baptism

Baptism is the sacrament that makes us children of God and members of the Body of Christ, the Church. Baptism takes away original sin and all personal **sin**. It unites us to Jesus and makes us temples of the Holy Spirit. In Baptism we celebrate God's promise that he will live in friendship with us forever.

God Loves Us

Faith Focus

How does God show his love for us?

God called Saint Paul to tell people about his love. Paul answered God's call and traveled to many cities to bring God's message. In the city of Athens, Paul stood up in the marketplace and spoke these words:

Scripture

ACTS 17:16–34

God Gives Everyone Life

"People of Athens!" Paul said. "I want to tell you about the one true God so that you can come to know him. He made the world and all that is in it. He is the Lord of heaven and earth. He gives everyone life and breath. He made everyone and everything, and he gave us the seasons of the year. He wants people to search for him and to find him in his creation."

Then Paul said, "It is not difficult to find God. He is near. We live and move and have our being in him."

"We are his children. God made us to be one family. He calls us to turn to him with love."

"He even sent his own Son, Jesus, to tell us how much he loves us and to show us how to live."

Some of the Greeks believed what Paul told them and became followers of Jesus.

BASED ON ACTS 17:16–34

? **What does Paul teach about God?**

? **How do you answer God's call to love him?**

Share

Write about God's love In the space below, write a sentence about one way God shows his love for you.

_____

_____

Signs of God's Love

SIGNS OF FAITH

The Holy Trinity

The mystery of one God in three Persons: Father, Son, and Holy Spirit is called the **Trinity** (*CCC*. Glossary). Each Person can be called God. Belief in the Trinity is the most important part of our faith. When we make the Sign of the Cross, we are saying we believe in the Trinity.

Faith Focus

What are the sacraments?

From the very beginning, God wanted people to be friends with him. He shared his life with humans. But the first humans turned away from God's friendship. They disobeyed him and sinned. We call this first sin **original sin**. Original sin affects all people. Because of it, suffering came into the world and people tend to sin.

Even after the first humans turned away from him, God still wanted to live in friendship with people. So God our Father sent his Son, Jesus, to show us how much he loves us. Jesus is the most important sign of God's love.

- Jesus showed us how to live in friendship with God.

- Jesus died on the cross to save us from sin.

- Jesus showed us that even when we turn from God's friendship, God will forgive us.

The Sacraments of Initiation

Jesus gave us the sacraments so we would know God's love, forgiveness, healing, and call to service. A **sacrament** is an outward sign that comes from Jesus. The seven sacraments give us grace.

Baptism is the first of the three Sacraments of Initiation. In Baptism we are united to Jesus and receive new life. In Confirmation the Holy Spirit gives us strength to live as followers of Jesus. Baptism and Confirmation mark us with a special character, so we can only receive them once.

In the Eucharist we receive the Body and Blood of Jesus. We can participate in the Eucharist often. The Eucharist helps us be more like Jesus. It helps us live and move and have our being in God.

These three sacraments together make us members of the Church. The Church is a sign of God's love. God calls us to live in community with other people who believe in him. The Church family helps us grow as God's children.

❓ **What are some signs of God's love in your life?**

Being a Member

Respond

Write about being a member Write a sentence in the banner to tell how you show you are a member of the Church. Then decorate your banner.

Closing Blessing

Gather and begin with the Sign of the Cross.

Leader: God, our Father, you give us all the living creatures.

All: We praise and thank you.

Leader: Jesus, our Savior, you give us life.

All: We praise and thank you.

Leader: Holy Spirit, our Helper, you make us holy.

All: We praise and thank you.

Leader: Let us go forth in peace and love.

All: Thanks be to God.

Sing together.

We are called to act with justice,
we are called to love tenderly.
We are called to serve one another,
to walk humbly with God!

We Are Called, © David Haas, GIA Publications

Faith at Home

Faith Focus

- In Baptism God calls us to a life of happiness with him.
- A sacrament is an outward sign that comes from Jesus and gives us grace.
- Jesus is the greatest sign of God the Father's love.

Ritual Focus

Signing with the Cross The celebration focused on being signed with holy water. The children came to the water, were called by name, and signed with the Sign of the Cross. During the week, bless your child by signing him or her with the Sign of the Cross each day at a convenient time for both of you.

GO ONLINE **www.harcourtreligion.com**
Visit our Web site for weekly scripture readings and questions, family resources, and more activities.

Act

Share Together Read Isaiah 43:1–4. Invite family members to share how the reading makes them feel. Then talk together about the words, "I have called you by name, you are mine." Invite family members to share why they have the names they do. Then ask individuals to share what they like about their names. Ask everyone to be still and imagine God saying each of their names and adding, "You are mine."

Do Together God calls us to live in harmony with nature and to enjoy it. Choose one of the following to do as a family this week: Go on a nature walk. Discuss how your family can be stewards of water. Find an environmental project to become involved in, or volunteer to help take care of an elderly neighbor's yard.

Family Prayer

God, our Father, thank you for calling us to be your children. We know your love, and we want to share it with others. Send your Holy Spirit to help us love and care for everything you have created. We ask this in the name of your Son, Jesus. Amen.

2 We Are Welcomed

We Gather

Procession

As you sing, walk forward slowly. Follow the people carrying the Bible and candle. Gather around the candle.

🎼 Sing together.

We are marching in the light of God,
   we are marching in the light of God.
We are marching, we are marching
   in the light of God.
We are marching, we are marching
   in the light of God.

South African Traditional

Leader: Let us pray.

Make the Sign of the Cross together.

Ritual Focus: Renewal of Baptismal Promises

Leader: Jesus is the Light of the World.

Light the candle.

Leader: Let us renew our baptismal promises now.

Do you reject sin so as to live in the freedom of God's children?

All: I do.

Leader: Do you reject Satan, and all his works, and all his empty promises?

All: I do.

Leader: Do you believe in God, the Father almighty; in Jesus Christ, his only Son, our Lord; in the Holy Spirit and the holy catholic Church?

All: I do.

Leader: Sprinkle children with water.

Make the Sign of the Cross as you are sprinkled with holy water.

We Listen

Leader: Good and gracious Father, send us the Holy Spirit to open our hearts to the good news of your Son, Jesus, the Light of the World. We ask this in his name.

All: Amen.

Leader: A reading from the holy Gospel according to Luke.

All: Glory to you, Lord.

Leader: Read Luke 19:1–10.

The Gospel of the Lord.

All: Praise to you, Lord Jesus Christ.

Sit silently.

We Go Forth

Leader: Loving Father, thank you for the Light of Christ. Send us the Holy Spirit to help us live as children of the light.

All: Amen.

 Sing the opening song together.

13

The Light of Christ

SIGNS OF FAITH

Holy Water

Water blessed by a **priest** or deacon is called **holy water**. It is a sign of cleansing from sin when the water is sprinkled on the assembly. It may be sprinkled on the assembly at Sunday Mass, especially during the Easter season. We use holy water to make the Sign of the Cross and remember our Baptism as we come into church.

Reflect

Renewal of Baptismal Promises   Draw and write about one way that you can march in the Light of Christ.

_____

_____

_____

_____

Children of the Light

At Baptism we receive a candle. The priest or deacon prays that we will walk as children of the light. We are children of the light when we love and care about other people.

Sometimes we do not act like children of the light. Even though we love our family, we may do things that are unkind. We may hurt our friends. Sometimes we choose not to care about what others want or need. We choose sin.

We know what it is like to do something wrong. We know what it is like to feel sorry and want to make up. What if we never got a second chance?

Candles

Candles are signs of Christ, the Light of the World. Candles are used at the altar during Mass. The most important candle used in the sacraments is the **Paschal candle**. This candle is blessed at the Easter Vigil and burned during the Masses of the Easter season. It is also burned at Baptisms and funerals throughout the year. Sometimes candles are placed before the altars of Mary and the saints. These candles are a sign of respect and prayer.

Jesus Brings Good News

Faith Focus

What happens when Jesus welcomes us?

Jesus welcomed sinners. He ate and drank with them. He gave them a second chance. He told them stories about God. He healed and forgave them. When people got to know Jesus, they changed.

Scripture

LUKE 19:1–10

Zacchaeus

One day Jesus was going through the town of Jericho. The crowds gathered to see him. He did not plan to stop there. On his way through the town, Jesus looked up into a sycamore tree. There in the branches was a man! It was Zacchaeus.

Zacchaeus was a rich tax collector and a sinner. He really wanted to see Jesus. He climbed the tree because he was so short that he could not see Jesus.

When Jesus saw Zacchaeus, he said, "Zacchaeus, come down quickly, for today I must stay at your house." Zacchaeus came down quickly and welcomed Jesus to his house with joy. He was very happy.

The people in the crowd were not happy. They said, "He has gone to stay at the house of a sinner." They did not think Jesus should be around sinners.

Zacchaeus told Jesus, "I will give half of my possessions to the poor. If I have taken anything from anyone, I will pay them back four times more."

Jesus said, "Zacchaeus, today God's forgiveness has come to your house."

BASED ON LUKE 19:1–10

? **Why do you think Jesus decided to stop at Zacchaeus' house?**

? **How would you feel if Jesus came to your home? How would you change?**

Faith at Home

Read the scripture story with your child. Discuss responses to the questions. Point out the effect Jesus had on Zacchaeus. Emphasize Jesus' welcoming gesture to Zacchaeus and how Jesus invited himself into Zacchaeus' home. Talk about ways your family welcomes people.

Share

Get ready   In the space below, write one thing you would do if Jesus came to your home.

_____

_____

_____

Second Chance

SIGNS OF FAITH

Reconciliation Room

The place where individuals celebrate the Sacrament of Reconciliation with the priest is called a **Reconciliation room**. The room is set up so we can sit face-to-face with the priest, or we may choose to kneel or sit behind a screen while we speak to him. The priest cannot ever tell what we say to him during the Sacrament of Reconciliation.

Faith Focus

How are we welcomed in the Sacrament of Reconciliation?

When God created us, he gave us free will. This is the ability to choose between right and wrong. When we choose to do what we know is wrong, we sin.

One of the ways we can show we are sorry for our sins and ask God's forgiveness is in the **Sacrament of Reconciliation**. We also call this the **Sacrament of Penance**, the Sacrament of Forgiveness, or Confession.

We can celebrate this sacrament again and again. It is necessary to do so when we choose to turn away from God's love and separate ourselves from God's life. This is called a **mortal sin**. For a sin to be mortal, it must be seriously wrong, we must know it is seriously wrong, and we must freely choose to do it anyway. We can also receive this sacrament for less serious sins that weaken our friendship with God. A less serious sin is called a **venial sin**.

Preparation and Welcome

The Church celebrates Penance in two ways. In **individual celebrations** the person seeking forgiveness meets alone with the priest. In **communal celebrations** groups of people gather to listen to God's word and pray. Then each person tells his or her sins privately to the priest.

In the Sacrament of Reconciliation the priest acts in the place of Jesus. The priest is a sign of God's forgiveness. He prepares to welcome us to the Sacrament of Penance by praying to the Holy Spirit. He asks the Holy Spirit to help him tell us about God's love and forgiveness.

We prepare for the sacrament by praying to the Holy Spirit and looking at our actions. We begin with the Sign of the Cross. In an individual celebration, the priest then greets us with words like these: "May God who has enlightened every heart help you to know your sins and trust in his mercy." We answer, "Amen."

❓ **How will you ask the Holy Spirit to help you look at your life?**

Preparing to Celebrate

Respond

Write a letter   In the space below, write a short letter telling God how you feel about preparing for your first celebration of the Sacrament of Reconciliation.

_____

_____

_____

_____

_____

Closing Blessing

Gather and begin with the Sign of the Cross.

Leader: God, our Gracious Father, you welcome us as your children. Increase our faith and make us strong.

All: Hear us, we pray.

Leader: God, our Gracious Father, you call us to change and grow. Make our light burn brighter for you.

All: Hear us, we pray.

Leader: God, our Gracious Father, help us to know our sins and trust in your mercy.

All: Hear us, we pray.

♪ Sing together.

We are marching in the light of God,
   we are marching in the light of God.
We are marching, we are marching
   in the light of God.
We are marching, we are marching
   in the light of God.

South African Traditional

Faith at Home

Faith Focus

- At Baptism we are called to walk in the light.
- Sin is a choice.
- The Sacrament of Reconciliation forgives sins committed after Baptism.

Ritual Focus

Renewal of Baptismal Promises The celebration focused on the Renewal of Baptismal Promises and sprinkling with holy water. The children renewed their baptismal promises and were sprinkled with holy water. During the week, use the text on page 12 and renew your own baptismal promises with your child and the rest of the family.

Act

Share Together Read Luke 19:1–10. Talk about what it must have been like for Zacchaeus to have Jesus come to his house. Point out the changes Zacchaeus made after he met Jesus. Then invite each family member to list people whose example caused some change in his or her own life. Ask each person to read the names on the list. After each name, pray together, "God bless you for being a light in our lives."

Do Together Together, think about and share the names of some people that your family could contribute some light and joy to. Emphasize that even small things can brighten someone's day. Choose one of the people and plan what you will do to brighten his or her life.

Family Prayer

Loving Father, we give you thanks for all the ways you make yourself known to us. Help us to continue to spread the Light of Christ in our world. We ask this in the name of your Son, Jesus. Amen.

We Gather

Procession

As you sing, walk forward slowly. Follow the person carrying the Bible.

 Sing together.

> Misericordia, Señor,
>   show us your mercy, O Lord,
> hemos pecado,
>   for we have sinned.

Salmo 50: Misericordia, Señor/Psalm 51:Show Us Your Mercy,
Lord © Bob Hurd. Published by OCP

Leader: Let us pray.

Make the Sign of the Cross together.

We Listen

Ritual Focus: Reverencing the Word

Come forward one at a time. Bow or place your hand on the Bible.

Leader: [Name], may God's word always enlighten you.

Child: Amen.

Leader: God, our loving Father, you call us to holiness and goodness. You want us to be united in you. Send us the Holy Spirit so that our minds and hearts will be open to your word and the works of your goodness. We ask this through Jesus Christ our Lord.

All: Amen.

Leader: A reading from the holy Gospel according to Luke.

All: Glory to you, Lord.

Leader: Read Luke 10:25–28.

The Gospel of the Lord.

All: Praise to you, Lord Jesus Christ.

Sit silently.

Leader: Let us join in the prayer Jesus has taught us.

Pray the Lord's Prayer together.

We Go Forth

Leader: May the Lord bless us, protect us from all evil, and bring us to everlasting life.

All: Amen.

 Sing the opening song together.

God's Word

Bowing

Bending the head or body forward shows honor and adoration for God. We also bow in prayer when we want to ask for God's blessing. Sometimes we bow our heads to reverence the name of Jesus.

Reflect

Reverencing the Word Think and write about the celebration.

When I listened to God's word

_____

_____

_____

When I bowed and put my hand on the Bible

_____

_____

_____

God's word is like

_____

_____

_____

God Speaks to Us

We reverence the Bible because it is a holy book. It is God's own word. The Bible tells the story of God's love for his people. The stories of what Jesus said and did are in the Bible.

We hear stories from the Bible every Sunday at Mass. During the Sacrament of Reconciliation, we read or listen to stories from the Bible. These stories may be about God's forgiveness or how we are to live God's laws.

We also use the Bible before we celebrate the Sacrament of Reconciliation to help us look at our lives. We pray to the Holy Spirit to help us see if we are living according to the Ten Commandments, the Beatitudes, the life of Jesus, and Church teachings.

SIGNS OF FAITH

The Bible

The Bible is God's own word. Another name used for the Bible is **Scriptures**. The word *Scriptures* means "writings." God guided humans to write the stories in the Bible about his love and forgiveness. The Bible has two parts, the Old Testament and the New Testament. The Old Testament tells the story of God's love and forgiveness before Jesus came. The New Testament tells us what Jesus and his followers taught about God's love and forgiveness.

Loving God and Neighbor

Faith Focus

What is the greatest commandment?

We want to do the right thing. Commandments help us know the difference between right and wrong. When Jesus was on earth, people wanted to know which one of God's commandments was the greatest.

Scripture

LUKE 10:25–28

The Great Commandment

One day when Jesus was teaching in a small town, a man who studied the commandments asked him, "Teacher, what must I do to be happy with God forever?" Jesus answered with a question of his own. "When you study God's law, what does it tell you?" The man replied, "You shall love the Lord your God with all your heart, with all your being, with all your strength, and with all your mind, and your neighbor as yourself." Jesus said, "You are right. Do this and you will be happy with God forever."

BASED ON LUKE 10:25–28

The Ten Commandments sum up for us what is right and wrong. Out of love, God gave the Ten Commandments to the people of Israel and to us. Following the commandments helps people stay close to God.

The Ten Commandments are divided into the two parts of the Great Commandment. The first three commandments show us how we are to love God. The last seven show us how to love ourselves and others. When Jesus told the man he was right, he was telling him and us that love is the greatest commandment.

The Ten Commandments show us how to live as God wants us to live. They tell us how to love God, ourselves, and others. They show us the way to real happiness.

❓ **What was Jesus trying to tell the man?**

❓ **When does following a commandment make you happy?**

Share

Draw a picture On a separate sheet of paper, draw a picture of a time you followed the Great Commandment.

The Examination of Conscience

SIGNS OF FAITH

Precepts of the Church

Precepts of the Church are helpful laws made by the Church. They help us know the basic things we must do to grow in love of God and neighbor. A list of the precepts is on page 72.

Faith Focus

What happens during the examination of conscience?

When we prepare to receive the Sacrament of Reconciliation, we examine our conscience. Just as God gives us the gift of free will, he also gives us the gift of conscience. **Conscience** helps us know the difference between right and wrong, good and evil. It also helps us know whether something we already did was right or wrong. We need to pray and learn Jesus' teachings to make our conscience strong. This will help our conscience point us in the right direction.

Here are some questions we ask ourselves during the **examination of conscience**:

- Did I live as Jesus wants me to?
- Did I go to Mass on Sunday?
- Did I love and respect my family members?
- Did I share my time and things with others?
- Did I tell the truth, return others' belongings, and treat people fairly?

We Listen to God's Word

When we examine our conscience, we can use Scripture. We often listen to Scripture during the celebration of the Sacrament of Reconciliation. When we receive the sacrament individually, the priest may read the Scripture. Or he may ask us to read a scripture story.

When we celebrate the sacrament with the community, we begin with a Celebration of the Word of God. We listen to one or more readings, and the priest gives a homily. The readings and homily help us hear God's voice. They remind us that God wants to forgive us.

After the homily there is a period of silence. We prayerfully think about our lives.

❓ **Which scripture story will you choose for your examination of conscience?**

Faith at Home

Discuss your child's answer to the question. Use pages 68–69 in the back of this book to go over the guidelines for the examination of conscience.

Showing Love

Respond

Finish the prayer Finish the prayer by writing or drawing in each space.

Dear God,
I will show my love
for you by

I love others, too.
I will show my love
for others by

Closing Blessing

Gather and begin with the Sign of the Cross.

Leader: The Lord speaks words of forgiveness and love always. Let us ask him to open our minds and hearts to his love.

Open our hearts to your word that we grow ever closer to you.

All: We pray to you, hear us.

Leader: Teach us your ways, O Lord, that we may follow your law.

All: We pray to you, hear us.

Sing together.

Misericordia, Señor,
 show us your mercy, O Lord,
hemos pecado,
 for we have sinned.

Salmo 50: Misericordia, Señor/Psalm 51:Show Us Your Mercy, Lord © Bob Hurd. Published by OCP

Faith at Home

Faith Focus

- We prepare for the Sacrament of Reconciliation with an examination of conscience, using the word of God.

- The Holy Spirit guides us in examining our conscience.

- Conscience helps us know right from wrong.

Ritual Focus

Reverencing the Word The celebration focused on Reverencing the Word. The children honored God's word by bowing before the Bible or placing their hand on it while the catechist prayed that God's word would enlighten them. When you review the lesson's scripture story with your child, use the Leader's text on page 23 as a prayer before reading the story aloud. Continue to do this each week.

GO ONLINE **www.harcourtreligion.com**
Visit our Web site for weekly scripture readings and questions, family resources, and more activities.

Act

Share Together With your family, watch a favorite video, movie, or TV show. Afterward, discuss how the characters were or were not living the Great Commandment. Then ask family members to share examples of people they know who live this commandment well in their daily lives.

Do Together Do a prayerful communal examination of conscience with the whole family. Read the scripture story from this lesson. Invite family members to name times when one of you lived the Great Commandment. Decide one way your family will live out this commandment in the next week. Conclude by praying the Lord's Prayer.

Family Prayer

God, our Father, thank you for giving us the gift of conscience. Help us to be kind and helpful family members. Make us a family that loves you and all the people in our lives. Amen.

4 We Are Sorry

We Gather

Procession

As you sing, walk forward slowly. Follow the person carrying the Bible.

 Sing together.

> Remember your love and your
> faithfulness, O Lord.
> Remember your people and have
> mercy on us, Lord.

© 1973, 1978 Damean Music

Leader: Let us pray.

Make the Sign of the Cross together.

We Listen

Leader: Loving Father, send us the Holy Spirit to open our ears and hearts that we may hear your word and be filled with the courage to live it. We ask this through Jesus Christ our Lord.

All: Amen.

Leader: A reading from the holy Gospel according to Luke.

All: Glory to you, Lord.

Leader: Read Luke 7:36–38, 44–48, 50.

The Gospel of the Lord.

All: Praise to you, Lord Jesus Christ.

Sit silently.

Ritual Focus: **Examination of Conscience and Act of Contrition**

Leader: The sinful woman showed sorrow. Let us think about what we are sorry for.

During this quiet time, use these questions to examine your conscience.

Leader: Did I love and honor God?

Did I keep Sunday as a holy day?

Did I obey my parents?

Did I share with others?

Am I kind to others?

Did I tell the truth?

Let us pray.

Kneel.

All: My God, I am sorry for my sins with all my heart. In choosing to do wrong and failing to do good, I have sinned against you whom I should love above all things. I firmly intend, with your help, to do penance, to sin no more, and to avoid whatever leads me to sin. Our Savior, Jesus Christ, suffered and died for us. In his name, my God, have mercy.

Stand.

We Go Forth

Leader: Lord, our God, you know all things. We want to be more generous in serving you. Look on us with love and hear our prayer.

All: Amen.

Sorrow for Sin

SIGNS OF FAITH

Kneeling

Kneeling is a way we pray with our bodies. When we get on our knees, we are telling God that he is important to us. We depend on him. Kneeling is also a way of saying we are sorry for our sins and we want to be forgiven. It is a prayer of penitence.

Reflect

Examination of Conscience and Act of Contrition In the two sections below, draw a picture of yourself thinking about your actions and then telling God you are sorry.

Thinking about my actions

Telling God I am sorry

Ask for Forgiveness

When we are unkind to our friends or our family, we hurt our friendship with them. We feel sorrow or sadness. We wish we did not act that way. We want to make things right. We tell them that we are sorry for what we did. We promise not to do it again. We make up.

When we sin, we do things that hurt our friendship with God and others. When we examine our conscience, we pray to the Holy Spirit. The Holy Spirit helps us remember how much God loves us. We remember what a good friend Jesus is. The Holy Spirit helps us say to God and to others, "I am sorry. Please forgive me."

Contrition

Contrition is sorrow for sin. It is the first and most important action in the Sacrament of Penance. We are sorry for our sins because we have ignored or turned away from God. Sometimes we are sorry because of how much we love God. Other times we are sorry because we are afraid of being punished for what we did. Contrition makes us want to make things right again. We must have sorrow for our sins to receive the grace of the sacrament.

Sinners Come to Jesus

Faith Focus

How do people tell Jesus they are sorry?

When people heard Jesus' good news about God's love, they were sorry for their sins. They wanted to tell Jesus how sorry they were.

Scripture

LUKE 7:36–38, 44–48, 50

A Woman Who Was Sorry

Simon, a Pharisee, invited Jesus to have dinner with him. So Jesus went to Simon's home and sat at the table.

When a sinful woman in the town found out that Jesus was there, she bought an expensive jar of oil. She went to Simon's home and stood behind Jesus. She cried and started washing Jesus' feet with her tears and drying them with her hair. The woman kissed Jesus' feet and poured the oil on them.

Simon was surprised. He could not believe Jesus would let a sinner touch him. He wondered if Jesus knew that the woman was a sinner.

Jesus said to Simon, "Simon, I have something to say to you... When I came into your home, you did not give me water to clean my feet. But this woman has washed my feet with her tears and dried them with her hair. You did not greet me with a kiss, but she has not stopped kissing my feet. You did not anoint my head with oil, but she anointed my feet with expensive oil.

"So I tell you, her many sins have been forgiven. She has shown great love." Then Jesus said to the woman, "Your sins are forgiven... Your faith has saved you; go in peace."

BASED ON LUKE 7:36–38, 44–48, 50

❓ **How did the woman show Jesus she was sorry for her sins?**

❓ **How do you tell Jesus you are sorry?**

Faith at Home

Read the scripture story with your child. Discuss the responses to the questions. Talk about different ways family members can say they are sorry when they have done something wrong.

Share

Write a prayer Write your own prayer of sorrow to Jesus.

_____

_____

_____

The Confession of Sin

Penitent
A person who seeks forgiveness in the Sacrament of Penance is called a **penitent**.

Faith Focus

Why do we confess our sins?

The woman in the scripture story showed Jesus she was sorry for her sins. She wanted to be Jesus' friend. In the Sacrament of Reconciliation, we show we are sorry.

- We admit we have done something wrong. This is called **confession**. We must always confess our mortal sins before going to Holy Communion. It is good for us to confess our venial sins often. Confession always helps our friendship with God grow stronger.

- We say, "I am sorry." This is called contrition.

- We plan ahead, so we will not act unlovingly the next time. This is called firm purpose of amendment.

- We do the penance the priest gives us. A **penance** is a prayer or action that we do to show we are really sorry.

Sorrow and Penance

In the Sacrament of Reconciliation, we confess our sins to the priest. He is called the **confessor**. He acts as God's minister when he listens to our confession. We talk with the priest about how we can make things right and do better.

Then the priest gives us a penance. The penance may be doing a good act connected to the sin, such as returning stolen property. It may also be an action that shows that we are willing to change, such as being kind. Often it is saying prayers.

Doing the penance helps us take responsibility for our actions. It reminds us to think about how our choices might hurt others.

After we accept our penance, we pray an Act of Contrition. The Act of Contrition is a prayer of sorrow. We tell God we are sorry and want to do better. We ask God to help us avoid temptation.

❓ **How does confession help us?**

Faith at Home

Discuss the response to the question. Talk about the difference between someone just saying "I am sorry," and someone showing that he or she is really sorry. Use page 33 to help your child learn an Act of Contrition.

Showing Sorrow

Respond

Tell a story Tell a story about a time you were sorry. Draw a picture in each space. Write a sentence about each picture.

Closing Blessing

Gather and begin with the Sign of the Cross.

Leader: Lord, look on us and hear our prayer. Give us strength to turn away from sin.

All: Lord, hear our prayer.

Leader: Help us to be sorry for our sins and to change so we can do better.

All: Lord, hear our prayer.

Leader: Help us to trust in your goodness and to be your generous children.

All: Lord, hear our prayer.

♪ Sing together.

Remember your love and your faithfulness, O Lord.
Remember your people and have mercy on us, Lord.

© 1973, 1978 Damean Music

Faith at Home

Faith Focus

- The Holy Spirit helps us feel sorry for our sins.

- Sorrow for sin is an important part of the Sacrament of Reconciliation.

- A penance is a prayer or action given by the priest to help us show that we are really sorry.

Ritual Focus

Examination of Conscience and Act of Contrition   The celebration focused on the Examination of Conscience and Act of Contrition. The children spent quiet time thinking about their own actions. This week spend some quiet time with your child, and together use the questions on page 33 to review each day. Begin your quiet time with the Prayer to the Holy Spirit on page 74.

www.harcourtreligion.com
Visit our Web site for weekly scripture readings and questions, family resources, and more activities.

Act

Share Together   All of us use the phrase "I'm sorry." We use it when we bump into someone. We use it when we have hurt someone. We use it to respond to someone who tells us something sad. Discuss the different meanings of these words. Ask family members to think about a time they were sorry. Talk about how they let the person know they were sorry and what happened after they expressed their sorrow.

Do Together   As a family, read the Act of Contrition on page 33. Discuss each phrase of the prayer, and invite family members to give examples from their own lives of what each phrase means to them. Talk about different ways to make amends for wrongdoings. Then pray the Act of Contrition together.

Family Prayer

Loving Father, send your Holy Spirit to help us understand when our actions hurt others in our family. Give us the strength to tell God and one another we are sorry and to do better in the future. We ask this in Jesus' name. Amen.

We Gather

Procession

As you sing, walk forward slowly. Follow the person carrying the Bible.

 Sing together.

Children of God, in one family,
loved by God, in one family
And no matter what we do
God loves me and God loves you.

Children of God, © Christopher Walker. Published by OCP

Leader: Let us pray.

Make the Sign of the Cross together.

We Listen

Leader: Good and gracious Father, you, who are always ready to forgive us, send us the Holy Spirit. Open our hearts and minds to know your forgiving love. We ask this in the name of your Son, Jesus.

A reading from the holy Gospel according to Luke.

All: Glory to you, Lord.

Leader: Read Luke 15:11–24.

The Gospel of the Lord.

All: Praise to you, Lord Jesus Christ.

Sit silently.

Ritual Focus: Prayer Over the Children

Leader: In the scripture story, Jesus told us about a father who loved his son very much. The father watched and waited for him to come home. God, our Father, loves us too. Even when we turn from him, he waits to welcome us home.

Leader: One at a time, come forward to the prayer table.

Place your open hands on the head of each child.

[Name], God loves you and will always forgive you.

Child: Thanks be to God.

Leader: Let us ask God, our Father, to forgive us and free us from evil.

Pray the Lord's Prayer together.

We Go Forth

Leader: May the God of peace fill your hearts with every blessing. May he strengthen you with the gift of hope. May he grant you all that is good.

All: Amen.

🎼 Sing the opening song together.

Reconciliation

SIGNS OF FAITH

Laying on of Hands

Jesus used the gesture of laying hands on people when he was blessing or healing them. In the Sacrament of Reconciliation, the priest extends his hands or hand over the head of the penitent as he prays the prayer of forgiveness.

Reflect

Prayer over the Children Think of someone you need to forgive. Write about and draw what you will do to show your forgiveness to that person.

_____

_____

_____

_____

Brought Together Again

When we are unkind to others, we hurt our relationship with them. Our parents, grandparents, or teachers trust us to obey them. When we disobey them, they are disappointed in us.

Sometimes we do things that hurt our friendship with others. We want to make it better. We say, "I am sorry. "We also want to be forgiven. When they say, "I forgive you," we are one with them again. We are reconciled. **Reconciliation** means "bringing together again, or reuniting."

In the Sacrament of Penance, God is always ready to forgive us. Through the power of the Holy Spirit, we are reconciled with God and one another.

SIGNS OF FAITH

Heaven: Together Forever
God want us to be one with him. This is why he forgives us. People who do not confess mortal sins will be separated from God forever. God wants us to be happy with him forever in heaven. So we confess our sins and try to grow in holiness now. People who die in God's friendship will eventually share in the joy of heaven.

God Wants to Forgive

What does Jesus tell us about God's forgiveness?

Jesus welcomed sinners. He ate and drank with them. He healed them and he forgave their sins. He also told stories to help people understand how much God, his Father, wanted to forgive them.

Scripture

LUKE 15:11–24

The Forgiving Father

Jesus once told this story: A man had two sons. The younger son said to his father, "Father, give me the share of the family money which is mine." So the father divided the family money between his two sons.

After a few days the younger son left his father's house. He took all of his belongings and went to a faraway country. He wasted all of his money. Then he became so hungry that he thought about eating the food that farmers gave to pigs.

The son thought about the people who worked for his father. He knew they had enough to eat. He decided to go home. He wanted to tell his father he was sorry. He hoped his father would give him a job.

While the son was still a long way off, his father saw him. The father was so happy to see him! He ran to him and put his arms around him and kissed him.

The son said, "Father I have sinned against heaven and against you; I do not deserve to be called your son." But his father told the servants to prepare a party. He said, "Let us celebrate. This son of mine was lost, and has been found." Then the party began.

BASED ON LUKE 15:11–24

❓ **When the son returns, what does he want from the father?**

❓ **What does this story tell you about God?**

Faith at Home

Read the scripture story with your child. Discuss your child's responses to the questions. Talk about why forgiveness is sometimes difficult.

Share

Write a sentence Fill in the spaces below to complete a sentence about God's forgiveness.

God's forgiveness is like_____

because_____.

The Sacrament of Forgiveness

SIGNS OF FAITH

Purple Stole

A **stole** is a vestment the priest wears when celebrating the sacraments. The stole is a sign of the priest's obedience to God and of his priestly authority. During the Sacrament of Reconciliation, the priest wears a purple stole around his neck and over his shoulders. The color purple is a sign of penance.

Faith Focus

How are sins forgiven in the Sacrament of Reconciliation?

In the scripture story, the son tells his father what he has done wrong. He asks for forgiveness. The father forgives the son and then surprises him. He brings him back into the family. The son is reconciled.

There are many ways we share in God's forgiveness. The most important ways are in the sacraments, especially the Sacrament of Reconciliation. This sacrament does just what it says.

- It forgives our sins.
- It brings us back together with God in friendship.
- It brings us back to the Church and makes us stronger members.
- It brings us peace.
- It heals our relationships.
- It makes us one with all creation.

Forgiveness and Absolution

God forgives our sins in the Sacrament of Reconciliation through the ministry of the priest. We confess our sins, accept our penance, and pray an Act of Contrition. Then the priest extends his hands over us and prays this prayer of forgiveness:

God, the Father of mercies,
through the death and resurrection of his Son
has reconciled the world to himself and sent
the Holy Spirit among us
for the forgiveness of sins;
through the ministry of the Church
may God give you pardon and peace,
and I absolve you from your sins
in the name of the Father, and of the Son, and
of the Holy Spirit.

RITE OF PENANCE, 55

This prayer is the prayer of **absolution**. *Absolution* means "forgiveness." You receive God's forgiveness through the Church in the Sacrament of Reconciliation.

❓ **What happens in the Sacrament of Reconciliation?**

Faith at Home

Talk about each of the effects of the Sacrament. Review your child's response to the question on this page. Use pages 68–69 to review the Rite of Penance with your child.

Serving Others

Respond

Write a story   Tell how you will show forgiveness this week.

_____

_____

_____

_____

_____

_____

Closing Blessing

Gather and begin with the Sign of the Cross.

Leader: God, our Father, in your goodness, forgive us our sins.

All: Lord, hear our prayer.

Leader: Jesus, our Savior, welcome us and show us your mercy.

All: Lord, hear our prayer.

Leader: Holy Spirit, fill us with the gift of forgiveness, that we may forgive others as we are forgiven.

All: Lord, hear our prayer.

Sing together.

Children of God, in one family,
loved by God, in one family
And no matter what we do
God loves me and God loves you.

Children of God, © Christopher Walker. Published by OCP

Faith at Home

Faith Focus

- God is always ready to forgive us.

- God wants us to be one with him. *Reconciliation* means "bringing together again, or reuniting."

- Through the power of the Holy Spirit and the ministry of the priest, our sins are forgiven.

Ritual Focus

Prayer Over the Children The celebration focused on God's love and forgiveness. The children came forward and the catechist extended hands over each of their heads, reminding them that God loves and forgives them. They prayed the Lord's Prayer. During the week, use the text on page 73 to pray the Lord's Prayer together.

Act

Share Together Read the three stories in chapter 15 of the Gospel according to Luke. Explain that Jesus told these stories to show how much God loves sinners and wants to forgive them. Ask family members to share their responses to these questions: What is Jesus telling us about God? Which of the three stories do you like the best? Why?

Do Together Share some stories about individuals who were forgiven or forgave someone else. Talk about when it is hard to forgive others. Read Luke 15:11–24. Write a family prayer asking the Holy Spirit to help you be forgiving to one another. Pray the prayer together when you gather for meals, at bedtime, or before a family gathering.

Family Prayer

Dear God, you are so generous in your love for us. You always welcome us back. Help us to be generous in our forgiveness of others. Amen.

6 We Go Forth

We Gather

Procession

As you sing, walk forward slowly. Follow the person carrying the Bible.

 Sing together.

We're all coming back together
With our God and family.
We're all coming back together
Building the kingdom for everyone.
Building the kingdom for everyone.

© 2005 John Burland

Leader: Let us pray.

Make the Sign of the Cross together.

We Listen

Leader: Loving Father, we come together in your presence to remember that we are your children. You call us to be children of the light. Open our hearts to the Holy Spirit that we will understand your word. We ask this through Jesus Christ our Lord.

All: Amen.

Leader: A reading from the holy Gospel according to John.

All: Glory to you, Lord.

Leader: Read John 20:19–23.

The Gospel of the Lord.

All: Praise to you, Lord Jesus Christ.

Sit silently.

Leader: Jesus asks us to forgive others and to bring peace into the world. Through our Baptism and the Sacrament of Reconciliation, we are freed from sin and evil.

All: Amen.

Leader: Sprinkle the children with water.

You have been baptized in Christ, and you are called to bring his light to the world.

All: Amen. Alleluia!

Leader: Let us offer each other the Sign of Peace.

Offer one another a sign of Christ's peace.

Say: "The Peace of the Lord be with you."

Answer: "And also with you."

We Go Forth

Leader: God, our Father, send us the Holy Spirit, the giver of peace, that we may go forth as a people of peace and forgiveness.

All: Thanks be to God.

♪ Sing the opening song together.

53

We Share

Signs of Faith

Sprinkling with Holy Water

At some Sunday Masses during the Easter season, the priest walks through the church and sprinkles the assembly with holy water. The sprinkling reminds us of our Baptism. In Baptism, God forgives and heals us. When the priest does the sprinkling with water, it takes the place of the Penitential Rite.

Sprinkling with Water and the Sign of Peace Make a list of three things you do to bring Christ's light into the world.

1. _____

_____

_____

2. _____

_____

_____

3. _____

_____

_____

We Are Reconciled

We grow and change when we receive the Sacrament of Reconciliation. It is a sacrament of conversion. **Conversion** means "changing or moving away from one thing and toward another."

When we celebrate the Sacrament of Reconciliation, we name the things that have broken or hurt our relationship with God and others. We are sorry and want to change. We accept the penance the priest gives us to show this.

We receive God's forgiveness and peace. Through the action of the Holy Spirit, we are one again with God and others. We are reconciled and at peace.

SIGNS OF FAITH

Sign of Peace

During the Mass, we exchange the Sign of Peace before Holy Communion. The Sign of Peace is a sacred action. It is a sign that we are one in the Body of Christ. When we offer each other the Sign of Peace, we remember that we are all one.

Jesus Shares Peace and Forgiveness

REMEMBER

Faith Focus

What did Jesus send the disciples to do?

While he was alive, Jesus' disciples traveled, preaching and healing in his name. The Risen Jesus wanted them to carry on his work of healing and forgiveness.

Scripture

JOHN 20:19–23

Jesus Appears to the Disciples

On the evening of the first Easter, the disciples were together. They locked themselves in a room because they were afraid. They knew Jesus had risen from the dead. They thought the people who had put Jesus to death might come after them.

Suddenly Jesus appeared in the room. He said, "Peace be with you." The disciples were so happy to see him. Jesus again said, "Peace be with you. As the Father has sent me, so I send you."

After Jesus said, "Peace be with you," he breathed on the disciples and said to them, "Receive the Holy Spirit. Whose sins you shall forgive are forgiven them, and whose sins you do not forgive, they are not forgiven."

BASED ON JOHN 20:19–23

❓ **What do you think Jesus was sending the disciples to do?**

❓ **How are you forgiving of your friends?**

Faith at Home

Read the scripture story with your child. Discuss your child's responses to the questions. Talk about ways that forgiveness brings peace. Use examples from your family's life together.

Share

Draw a picture Show one way you bring forgiveness and peace to other members of your family.

Proclamation of Praise and Dismissal

SIGNS OF FAITH

Bishops and Priests

In a special way the Church continues Jesus' mission of forgiveness and reconciliation through the ministry of bishops and priests. Like the Apostles, bishops and priests receive from Jesus the authority to absolve people from their sins. They teach us how to live out the mission of reconciliation.

Faith Focus

How do we share reconciliation with others?

Jesus wanted his disciples to know they were forgiven. He wanted them to be at peace. They had a special job, a mission. He was sending them to make the world a better place. He wanted them to bring forgiveness and peace to others, just as he did. He was calling them to be reconcilers.

The Church continues the mission of reconciliation today. We are reconcilers when we do these things:

- forgive others

- ask for forgiveness

- are fair to others

- act with kindness

- share what we have with those who do not have

- respect all people because they are God's children

The mission of reconciliation is not always easy. The Holy Spirit gives us strength and courage to carry it out.

Go Forth

At the end of the celebration of Reconciliation, we give praise to God for his wonderful gift of forgiveness and reconciliation.

After the prayer of absolution, the priest says, "Give thanks to the Lord, for he is good." We respond, "His mercy endures for ever."

Then the priest sends us forth. He says,

> Go in peace,
> and proclaim to the world
> the wonderful works of God
> who has brought you salvation.

RITE OF PENANCE, 47

Our sins are forgiven in the Sacrament of Reconciliation. The Holy Spirit remains with us. He helps us grow and become more like Jesus. This is such a great gift that we want to tell the world about it. The best way we can do that is to be signs of God's forgiveness and reconciliation to others.

❓ **What can you do to be a sign of God's forgiveness and mercy?**

Faith at Home

Review your child's response to the question. Use page 45 to review the meaning of Reconciliation with your child.

Being a Reconciler

Respond

Fill in the circles In each of the blank circles, write one way you will be a reconciler this week.

I am a reconciler.

Closing Blessing

Gather and begin with the Sign of the Cross.

Leader: God and Father of us all, you forgive our sins.

All: Thank you for your forgiveness.

Leader: Jesus, our Savior, you give us the gift of peace.

All: Thank you for your peace.

Leader: Holy Spirit, you give us your strength and courage.

All: Thank you for your strength and courage.

🎵 Sing together.

> We're all coming back together
> With our God and family.
> We're all coming back together
> Building the kingdom for everyone.
> Building the kingdom for everyone.

© 2005 John Burland

Faith at Home

Faith Focus

- The Sacrament of Reconciliation is a sacrament of conversion.

- The mission of reconciliation is to bring forgiveness and peace to others.

- The Holy Spirit remains with us to help us grow and become more like Jesus.

Ritual Focus

Sprinkling with Water and the Sign of Peace   The celebration focused on bringing Christ's light and peace into the world. The children were sprinkled with water and extended a Sign of Peace to one another. During the week, at appropriate family gathering times, begin or end the gathering with a Sign of Peace.

GO ONLINE www.harcourtreligion.com
Visit our Web site for weekly scripture readings and questions, family resources, and more activities.

Act

Share Together   Read John 20:19–23, and discuss how the disciples must have felt when Jesus appeared to them. Reflect on how they had run away from Jesus during his Passion and death. But Jesus just said, "Peace be with you." Conclude with the Prayer of Saint Francis on page 74.

Do Together   During the next week, gather together, light a candle, and pray this prayer: "We have been baptized in Christ and called to bring his light to the world." Then ask family members to share one way they were a light to someone. Pray the Prayer to the Holy Spirit on page 74.

Family Prayer

Gracious God, we give you thanks and praise for the gifts of your mercy and forgiveness. Help us to go out and spread the word of your love to those we meet. Show us how to be reconcilers in our family and with our friends. Amen.

Words of Faith

absolution The forgiveness of sin that we receive from God through the Church in the Sacrament of Reconciliation.

Baptism The sacrament that makes the person a child of God and a member of the Church. It takes away original sin and all personal sin and makes the person a temple of the Holy Spirit.

communal celebration In a communal celebration, the assembly gathers to pray and hear God's word. Each penitent then confesses his or her sins to a priest, receives a penance, and is absolved individually.

confession Telling our sins to a priest in the Sacrament of Reconciliation. What we confess to the priest is private.

confessor A priest who acts as God's minister when he listens to our confession.

conscience God's gift which helps us know the difference between right and wrong. It also helps us recognize whether an action we already did was right or wrong.

contrition Sorrow for sins and a willingness to do better. Contrition is our first step toward forgiveness. As part of the Sacrament of Reconciliation, we pray an Act or Prayer of Contrition.

conversion A sincere change of mind, will, and heart away from sin and toward God. The Sacrament of Reconciliation is a sacrament of conversion.

examination of conscience A prayerful way of looking at our lives in light of the Ten Commandments, the Beatitudes, the life of Jesus, and the teachings of the Church. It helps us know whether what we have done is right or wrong.

grace A sharing in God's own life.

Holy Trinity The three Persons in one God: God the Father, God the Son, and God the Holy Spirit.

holy water Water blessed by the priest for a religious purpose.

individual celebration In an individual celebration, the penitent meets with the priest in the Reconciliation room. The penitent confesses his or her sins to the priest, receives a penance, and is absolved.

mortal sin A serious sin that separates us from God's life.

original sin The name given to the first sin of humans. Because they disobeyed God and turned away from his friendship, original sin is passed to all of us.

Paschal candle A candle that is blessed at Easter Vigil and is burned during the Masses of the Easter season. It is also burned at Baptisms and funerals throughout the year.

penance A prayer or good action that we do to show we are sorry for our sins and want to do better. In the Sacrament of Reconciliation, the priest gives us a penance.

penitent The person who confesses his or her sins to the priest in the Sacrament of Reconciliation.

Precepts of the Church Laws of the Church that help us know what we should do to grow in love of God and neighbor.

priest A man who is ordained to serve God and the Church by celebrating the sacraments, preaching, and presiding at Mass. The priest is the confessor, or minister of the Sacrament of Reconciliation. The stole is a sign of the priest's obedience to God and of his priestly authority.

R

reconciliation A coming back together.

Reconciliation room A room or chapel in which the confessor, or priest, hears the penitent's confession of sins. The room is usually furnished with chairs, a kneeler, a table for the Bible, and a candle. A movable screen can also be used as divider between the priest and the penitent.

S

sacrament An outward sign that comes from Jesus and gives us grace, a share in God's life.

Sacrament of Penance Another name for the Sacrament of Reconciliation.

Sacrament of Reconciliation A sacrament of forgiveness through which the sinner is reconciled with God and the Church.

Scriptures The word of God contained in the Bible. The word *Scripture* means "holy writing." Scripture is used for reflecting on God's love and forgiveness in the Sacrament of Reconciliation. Scripture is proclaimed by a lector, or reader, at Mass, at a communal celebration, or in other liturgical celebrations.

 **sin** The choice to disobey God. Sin is a deliberate choice, not a mistake or accident. We accept God's loving forgiveness for our sins when we show by our sorrow that we are willing to do better.

stole A vestment the priest wears around his neck when celebrating the sacraments.

venial sin A less serious sin that weakens our friendship with God.

Celebrating the Sacrament

The Communal Rite of Reconciliation

Before celebrating the Sacrament of Reconciliation, take time to examine your conscience. Pray for the Holy Spirit's help.

1. Introductory Rites

Join in singing the opening hymn. The priest will greet the assembly and lead you in the opening prayer.

2. Celebration of the Word of God

Listen to the word of God. There may be more than one reading, with a hymn or psalm in between. The last reading will be from one of the Gospels.

3. Homily

Listen as the priest helps you understand the meaning of the Scriptures.

4. Examination of Conscience, Litany, and the Lord's Prayer

After the homily there will be a time of silence. The priest may lead the assembly in an examination of conscience. This will be followed by a prayer of confession and a litany or song. Then everyone prays the Lord's Prayer together.

5. Individual Confession, Giving of Penance, and Absolution

While you wait to talk with the priest, you may pray quietly or join in singing. When it is your turn, confess your sins to the priest. He will talk to you about how to do better. He will give you a penance and extend his hands over your head and pray the prayer of absolution.

6. Proclamation of Praise and Dismissal

After everyone has confessed individually, join in the prayer or in singing a litany of thanksgiving. The priest or deacon will lead the closing prayer and bless the assembly. Then the priest or deacon will dismiss the assembly.

After celebrating the sacrament, carry out your penance as soon as possible.

The Individual Rite of Reconciliation

Before celebrating the Sacrament of Reconciliation, take time to examine your conscience. Pray for the Holy Spirit's help.

Wait for your turn to enter the Reconciliation room. You may choose to meet with the priest face-to-face or be separated from the priest by a screen.

1. Welcome

The priest will welcome you and invite you to pray the Sign of the Cross.

2. Reading of the Word of God

The priest may read or recite a passage from the Bible. You may be invited by the priest to read the Scripture yourself.

3. Confession of Sins and Giving of Penance

You tell your sins to the priest. The priest will talk with you about how to do better. Then the priest will give you a penance.

4. Prayer of the Penitent

Pray an Act of Contrition.

5. Absolution

The priest will hold his hand over your head and pray the prayer of absolution. As he says the final words, he will make the Sign of the Cross.

6. Proclamation of Praise and Dismissal

You and the priest praise God for his mercy, and the priest sends you forth.

After celebrating the Sacrament, carry out your penance as soon as possible.

Remember, after you celebrate this sacrament for the first time, you should receive it often to strengthen your friendship with God. We receive the Sacrament of Reconciliation before we receive Holy Communion for the first time. We are required to celebrate the Sacrament of Reconciliation once a year if we have committed mortal sin. We cannot receive Holy Communion if we have not received forgiveness for a mortal sin.

Sources of Morality

The Great Commandment

"You shall love the Lord your God with all your heart, and with all your soul, and with all your strength, and with all your mind; and your neighbor as yourself."

Luke 10:27

The New Commandment

"This is my commandment, that you love one another as I have loved you."

John 15:12

Love of Enemies

"But I say to you, Love your enemies and pray for those who persecute you, so that you may be children of your Father in heaven…."

Matthew 5:44–45

The Beatitudes

"Blessed are the poor in spirit,
    for theirs is the kingdom of heaven.

Blessed are those who mourn,
    for they will be comforted.

Blessed are the meek,
    for they will inherit the earth.

Blessed are those who hunger and thirst
    for righteousness,
    for they will be filled.

Blessed are the merciful,
    for they will receive mercy.

Blessed are the pure in heart,
    for they will see God.

Blessed are the peacemakers,
    for they will be called children of God.

Blessed are those who are persecuted for
    righteousness' sake,
    for theirs is the kingdom of heaven."

Matthew 5:3–10

The Ten Commandments

1. I am the Lord your God. You shall not have strange gods before me.	Put God first in your life before all things.
2. You shall not take the name of the Lord your God in vain.	Respect God's name and holy things. Do not use bad language.
3. Remember to keep holy the Lord's Day.	Take part in Mass on Sundays and holy days. Avoid unnecessary work on those days.
4. Honor your father and your mother.	Obey and show respect to parents and others who are responsible for you.
5. You shall not kill. Do not hurt yourself or others.	Take care of all life. Avoid anger, fighting, and being a bad example.
6. You shall not commit adultery.	Show respect for marriage and family life. Respect your body and the bodies of others.
7. You shall not steal.	Respect creation and the things that belong to others. Do not cheat. Do not take things that do not belong to you. Do not damage the property of others.
8. You shall not bear false witness against your neighbor.	Tell the truth. Do not gossip. Do not lie or hurt others' good reputations.
9. You shall not covet your neighbor's wife.	Be faithful to family members and friends. Do not be jealous. Avoid impure thoughts and actions.
10. You shall not covet your neighbor's goods.	Share what you have. Do not envy what other people have. Do not be greedy or desire other people's property.

Precepts of the Church

1. Take part in the Mass on Sundays and holy days. Keep these days holy, and avoid unnecessary work.

2. Celebrate the Sacrament of Reconciliation at least once a year if you have committed a serious, or mortal, sin.

3. Receive Holy Communion at least once a year during Easter time.

4. Fast and abstain on days of penance.

5. Give your time, gifts, and money to support the Church.

Works of Mercy

Corporal (for the body)

Feed the hungry.

Give drink to the thirsty.

Clothe the naked.

Shelter the homeless.

Visit the sick.

Visit the imprisoned.

Bury the dead.

Spiritual (for the spirit)

Warn the sinner.

Teach the ignorant.

Counsel the doubtful.

Comfort the sorrowful.

Bear wrongs patiently.

Forgive injuries.

Pray for the living and the dead.

Catholic Prayers

✳ The Sign of the Cross

In the name of the Father
and of the Son
and of the Holy Spirit
Amen.

✳ The Lord's Prayer

Our Father, who art in heaven,
hallowed be thy name;
thy kingdom come;
thy will be done on earth as it is in heaven.
Give us this day our daily bread;
and forgive us our trespasses
as we forgive those who trespass against us;
and lead us not into temptation,
but deliver us from evil.
Amen.

Hail Mary

Act of Contrition

My God,
I am sorry for my sins with all my heart.
In choosing to do wrong
and failing to do good,
I have sinned against you
whom I should love above all things.
I firmly intend, with your help,
to do penance,
to sin no more,
and to avoid whatever leads me to sin.
Our Savior Jesus Christ
suffered and died for us.
In his name, my God, have mercy.

Confiteor

I confess to Almighty God
and to you, my brothers and sisters,
that I have sinned through my own fault,
in my thoughts and in my words,
in what I have done,
and in what I have failed to do;
and I ask Blessed Mary ever virgin,
all the angels and saints,
and you, my brothers and sisters,
to pray for me to the Lord our God.

Prayer of Saint Francis of Assisi

Lord, make me an instrument of your peace.
Where there is hatred, let me show love;
where there is injury, pardon;
where there is doubt, faith;
where there is despair, hope;
where there is darkness, light;
and where there is sadness, joy.

O Divine Master, grant that I may not so
     much seek
to be consoled as to console;
to be understood as to understand;
to be loved as to love.
For it is in giving that we receive;
it is in pardoning that we are pardoned;
and it is in dying that we are born to
     eternal life.
Amen.

Prayer to the Holy Spirit

Come, Holy Spirit, fill the hearts of your
     faithful
And kindle in them the fire of your love.
Send forth your Spirit and they shall be
     created.
And you shall renew the face of the earth.

An Examination of Conscience

1. You prepare for the Sacrament of Reconciliation by thinking about the things you have done or not done. Think about how you have followed the Beatitudes, the Ten Commandments, and the Great Commandment.

2. Pray to the Holy Spirit to be with you as you think about your choices and actions.

3. Ask yourself:
   - Did I use God's name with respect?
   - Did I show my love for God and others in some way?
   - Did I usually say my daily prayers?
   - Did I always obey my mother and father?
   - Was I kind to those around me or was I mean?
   - Was I fair in the way that I played and worked with others?

   - Did I share my things with others?
   - Did I avoid taking what belongs to someone else?
   - Did I care for my own things and others' things?
   - Did I hurt others by calling them names or telling lies about them?
   - Did I go to Mass and take part in the celebration?

4. Pray for the Holy Spirit's help to change and follow Jesus' example of love.

Boldfaced numbers refer to the pages on which the terms are defined. Many of these words are also defined in the Words of Faith section, pp. 62-67.

Hail Mary
Full of Grace
The Lord is with you!
Blessed are you among women,
and blessed is the fruit
of your womb Jesus.
Holy Mary, Mother of God,
pray for us sinners,
now and at the hour of our death.
Amen.